No Matter Where You Go, There You Are

Cliff Hahn

BookLeaf Publishing
India | USA | UK

Made with ❤ on the BookLeaf Publishing Platform
www.bookleafpub.in
www.bookleafpub.com

Dedication

To mom and dad: without you I wouldn't be here.

Preface

Poems from back then, until right now.

Acknowledgements

Thanks to all the dogs I've known before.

Delaware Peninsula

Remember the
snake mounds on Arrowhead Hill
where two low rivers join
where the last tribe of the Lenape
were vanquished by Clear People
who brought their Burger King
and Dairy Queen
to build build build
plasterboard shithouses
on hallowed ground
carved like flesh into
small perfect slabs
called Real Estate

Nuuanu Soiled

Digging these haole hands
into the mud
of my hardware-store-bought flower bed
realizing deep down
it's the exact same dirt, exact same spot
Hawaiians farmed only 100 years ago
harvesting taro and breadfruit
along the still flowing auwai
"my" auwai now
because Bank of America says so
"property owner shall not obstruct the irrigation
channel, above or below the property line"
as if the Night Marchers are coming back
to push me over the pali
to rip out my invasive butterfly bush
set fire to my redwood gazebo
and burn
all this
to the ground

Embrace the Warm

Went for a dip in Microplastic Bay
Swimming with water bottles, beach toys, white coral
Acidic ocean was lovely, like bathwater
(OK, more like toilet water)

Took a hike in Burning Forest
Surrounded by sounds of crackling trees
Smoky and quiet, just sick birds, so peaceful
(LOL, we are all Burning Man)

Paddled into town, kayaking on flooded streets
Returned a bunch of crap to Amazon
Garbage in, garbage out; waste more, want more
(Consuming ourselves to death)

Fun day in the park with my companion robot
Ate synthetic ice cream and real hot dogs
The zoo is awesome now
(All the animals are taxidermied)

It's the end of the world as we know it
And I feel fine

Peace in Your Time

"Dear Alien, come on down!"

and he entered the frame
and he entered the fray
he and his shiny, skinny little friends
made up of microphones, video lights
and big, teardrop-shaped hi-def eyes with crosshair eyesights

vaporized the bad stuff out of our sky
melted down the uranium, the guns and the carbon dioxide
declared

PEACE IN YOUR TIME

i guess
for a time

asking themselves
WHY WHY WHY?
and saying to each other
LOOK HOW THIS HAPPENED
and

OH MY, OH MY

they seemed a bit *too* inquisitive to me
holding us up for the whole universe to see
studying our every mistake
like some triumphant fifth estate

then tear-drops blazed with searing light;
then pale gray fingers,
long and taking flight,
held out our last hope
before – unbelievably – a joke,
one final jab:
"CAN'T HAVE THE MONKEYS DESTROYING THE LAB!"

the Blue and the Gray finally shook hands
with a few humbled earthmen,
then left with lights blinding,
with bug-eyed journalists reminding
PEACE IN YOUR TIME

at least
for a time

Sea Breeze

keep a watch out for my love
a twisted cupid thirsty for blood
left a trail of poisoned semen
stretched out all along the LIE
leading right into Montauk Harbor
where there's a big whirlpool
off your starboard side
out of control
out of desperation
i pull you deeper
and you and you and you and you and
somebody better put me down
before i drown
before i kill again

lost in fathomless sleep
daydreams and nightmares fuse
like barnacles to a sunken reef
dream a widow walking
above our nuclear family
now energetic & glowing
high on the hill overlooking Shoreham Bay
two love boats pass in the radiant night
signal warning

go down without ever knowing
why they sink
why they die

an American Sportsman
casting back out into open sea
i catch twenty two
including you
your heart gasping, flopping on the deck
sparkling in the sun like a sailfish shellacked
but i'm not laughing
i'm not sportsman proud
this disgusts me
this senseless carnage
caused by me, Captain Confusion,
casting hooks in every fucking direction
one-quarter Fish one-quarter Man
hoping to catch or be caught
hoping someone will never let me get away
with this again

terrified of rejection –
a Chicken of the Sea –
i'll return you first
and you'll thank me later
in a salty telegram
left tacked outside the harbor bar

in Oyster Bay, Southampton or Seaview
a bit sad, condescending and finally ending
“p.s. asshole, i loved you”

in long winters ahead
i'll sit 'round an electric fire
with bitter, smelly mates
eating “Sea Legs, The Vegetarian's Delight”
trading reformed fisherman's tales
of pitiful conquests and pseudo insight
like "was it worth it, was it right?"

and a single, stupid story
about the beauty i threw back tonight

See World

she took me down
the first bite of the revolution
to the bottom of the pool
were fed and were fed up
Sea World, a subsidiary of Harcourt Brace Jovanovich,
perhaps our equals in intelligence
Channel 7 was there on a beautiful Saturday
as blood rose to the surface
children screamed
jumping through hoops of fire
but i love animals
were fed and were fed up
live like a human in a closet
but i love animals
incidents happening more
book publishers
they let us ride them bareback
Shamu
wrote the first chapter of the revolution
and more often
were fed and were fed up
she took me to the bottom of the pool
but i love animals
she took me to the bottom of the pool

Shrink Wrapped

we all wait too patiently
patients slouch droopy
loopy in our overheated waiting room
HIP to be square to be there

then like a dearth of fresh air
Lilly white sales reps
powered by polyester pantsuits
march through
like they own the place
and they do
overflowing sample goodie bags
clutched by Lee Press On Nails
now in designer colors:
Prozac pink, Effexor green and Zoloft blue
no appointment needed
they stride into the inner chambers
led by Chubby the security guard
suddenly alert

now inert
i soon hear the door swing open again
as laughter spills out into the room
giving the clinic a clinic in irony

Chubby, doctors and secretaries re-emerge
waddling past with chocolate mousse pie, brie and
strawberries
i depress in the chair more than before
an appointment more delayed
and more pointless

gazillions of guinea pigs on a trillion-dollar wheel
spun with promises from pretty pill prescriptions and –
HMOw! –
hamsters like me
neither natured nor nurtured
wait in this stifling glass cage
stupidly straining for the feeder bottle of snake oil
mass-produced by lobbyists, researchers and marketers
from DC, Triangle Park and Madison Avenue

the healthiest thing i could do right now
is get up
stand right up on my hind legs
and bite the hand of the man that says
'talk to the hand'
demand my piece of the chocolate pie
but i'd lose my place in the feed line
pill cup outstretched
'please hook me up again'
if i can't

ever be happy
let me
ever be hopeful

Carolina On My Mind

i never forgot
that your father builds nuclear submarines
for the defense department.
the irony doesn't escape me,
it washes over my eyes,
burning with your White Linen perfume.

when you say
"why worry about the government?"
i worry about small p politics,
human politics,
abdications of self-rule.

no doubt greensboro is pretty in spring,
dogwoods showing off their colors,
"christ's colors" you said,
pink and white and red;
i would love to come down and visit but

it seems you'd rather forget about those people
who were murdered one summer by swastikas,
by linen.
and i can understand
how hoods are pulled over eyes.

Salem Witch

Mommy
I'm a big boy now
Tall enough to see above the kitchen table
I can watch you and your friend Cook
Playing cards, drinking Coke,
Smoking Salems

I like watching the pretty white smoke
Rise slowly from the ashtray
Curving, twisting, playing with the air
I see a clown, I see a tiger,
I see a funny face

I blow the air and make the smoke shape-shift
The funny face looks like a witch now
Swallowing my face
Burning my nose
I squeeze shut my eyes

Mommy
Witch says smoke will take away your friend
Smoke will burn down her house
Gunsmoke will take her husband too
Smoke will take away your daughter

Smoke will eat up your body
Smoke will take you away too
Goddamned smoke will take away everything here
Ashes to ashes, but first there will be smoke

I force open my eyes
And watch the white smoke
Twisting like a ghost dancer in the wind
A tight pirouette at the end of my joint
As I sit
Adult and alone

Daddy Sludge

One memory allowed:
I'm six, in your truck; your oily hands, oily rags.
But I liked the smell of diesel fuel.

At the very end of life for transmission oil,
after the oil has been reanimated through
countless phases of industrial recycling,
it finally is left as a viscous turd –
a blue-black bruise,
a glistening mound of gooey waste.
Useless Sludge.
That was you.

No smell, no taste, no sound;
you don't even feel.
Did you exist and, what for?

Subtracting your zinc,
your sulfur and phosphorus,
your cruelty, narcissism and sickness,
what remains of your remains?
Sludge.
Useless Sludge.

When I look at it now, I want to turn the lights down because I can see my reflection.

PS - so, how's death?

Human Errer

i was just an innocent by stand her
a pass her by
a witting witness
as they ate up
her delicate construction
getting the hemline
caught in the spaces
just under the hardhats
just between the eyeballs

i was an accidental inspect her
my only thought was
“just don't forget you're working that crane, pal!”

it was reported
as "human errer"
and no doubt he felt very guilty
but i thought i caught
a few of them
sneaking a last look
at her still perfect, untouched legs
jutting out from a mound of rubble

Fossil Fools

A PALEONTOLOGIST DINOSAUR
RUN INTO THE GROUND BY
ENDLESS HAND WRINGING
ABOUT YOUR HAND RINGING
DIGGING AND DYING,
UNEARTHING AND
LABELING,
THE FEW
PERSONAL
REMAINS
OF
WHAT
WAS
ME...

NOW EVOLVED:
NOW A SALARIMAN,
NOW A ROBOTNIK,
NOW A SEXUAL INSTAMATIC,
TAKING YOUR ELECTROMAGNETIC PULSE,
STOLEN WITH MY HAMFISTED METHODS,
AND SECRETED AWAY BETWEEN SOFT WHITE
SHEETS
OF COMPUTER PAPER, READING:

TWO HUMAN BEINGS,
FOSSIL FUELED BY
A SWEET & STICKY POWER LUNCH,
PRODUCE A REAL GREENHOUSE EFFECT:
REMOVAL OF YOUR OZONE LAYER,
MELTING OF MY POLAR ICECAP,
THE OCEANS BOIL AS WE
OVERLOOK THE RAMIFICATIONS
OF OUR DAMNING EMOTIONAL ENVIRONMENT
FIRING US INTO BONES OF MEMORY
FOREVER SEARED INTO STONE

Pixel

a sensuous, technicolor world
of music, of paperbacks, of cinemas,
of sitting aimlessly on a park bench,
began fading
began de
grading
in the 1996 Panix
the first login
ate my noggin
steadily dim
inishing
de
flating
down
to
this
flat
earth,
to
one
tiny
squ
are
do

t,

a

pi

x

el

now

look

ing

like

this:

.

Ub My REE

Rarest of rare earth elements,
You're off the charts –
Praseodymium is green with envy,
Lanthanum crawled back under a rock,
Even Neodymium wants to be your twin.

I get no kick from Thulium,
Mere Dysprosium doesn't thrill me at all,
So tell me
Why should it be true
That I get a kick out of you?

Sure, Scandium can fly me to the moon,
And, ho-hum, Holmium is bright as laser light.
Yeah, Yttrium can cause a spark,
And Samarium très sexuel magnétique?
I say couci-couça –
Cause I'd give the Earth for you.

Fear of Feeling

INTELLECTUAL HIJINX
HAVE HIJACKED
MY TRUE EMOTIONS
SOUTH OF THE BORDER
WHERE THEY
CAN NOW
BE SEEN
ON RADAR

Blackout

the ghost deck of the Love Boat
rises soggy from the syndicated sea
dozens of sunken-faced actors
small talking, selling instant coffee
not knowing the difference between
whole and whitebread
dying and dead

TURN ON, TUNE IN, DROP OUT
NO MORE RERUNS
AFTER THE BLACKOUT

I've seen you on fire in the river
red wet clay caked to your breasts
talking to a cowboy in chaps
armed with marketing stats
cable running out from under
his multi-purpose hat

HOOK UP! LOOK OUT!
GONNA DUMP SOME DVDs
ON YOUR VILLAGE
AFTER THE BLACKOUT

we are a teenage media mess
making sloppy wet electric connections
in the back seat of a tv truck
in :15 and :30 bites
within videos of legs and lips
digits and clips
magnetic particles
of true love get lost
now
before the Blackout

Hearts

I KNOW,
NO ONE HAS INNOCENCE.
BUT WE ARE.
YOUR ROMANTIC NOTIONS
OF TENDER RED TOMORROWS,
PINK CANDIES,
HEARTS PROTECTED
IN FORMALDEHYDE,
SECONDARY,
TO THIS REALISM
WE NEED:
HOT-RED FACES AND
BLACK-BRUISED EGOS
THAT ARE PAINFUL,
AUTHENTIC,
AND THEREFORE,
MORE APPEALING.

Kinetic Properties Of Sound

In a recent controversial experiment
a noted woman researcher
demonstrated the kinetic properties
of pure sound:

Words cut flesh,
noise made matter shrink,
syllables destroyed structures
that took years to build.

For the experiment,
the female technician
used the following phrases
on a test subject:
"I am leaving you"
"I don't love you anymore"
and
"I am moving to Texas with your cousin Dave"

These findings may be proclaimed as new
however further research indicates
these properties are as old
as man and woman
and man

QWERTY as Hell

we all lay out:
u next to i
i next to u
just .75 inches to the right

no shift needed,
underlining or italicizing
,though stylish,
unnecessary

then u were on top of j.
...but y?
and...k2 below u?? what the h.!?

o,
 y u & i, o y?

Mixed Candies

beautifully wrapped
heart-shaped box
assorted hard candies
sometimes outside sweet,
sometimes inside salty
sometimes sour shell,
so sweet in the middle

soft or hard?
i can't tell
until teeth breaks rock or
tongue tastes taffy

you make my mouth melt
or pierce my heart
guess i'm addicted to the sugar

Earth Ark

Where you gonna be
When the iceberg hits?
Because it will hit
You will suffer its violent jolt
Whether you are in the dark of the hold
Or standing with me
On the ship's bow
Giving witness

It has already begun
The ripping of the hull
The fires, the COVID
Bye-bye bees
And trees
And frogs
And bats
And coral
And dolphins (thanks for all the fish!)

All, all, even now, burned and swallowed
By Gaia's acidic sea
Zealandia won't be the only drowned continent
Welcome to scorched Atlantis

Do we go down with eyes wide shut
Glued to our screens
Just Netflix and grill
Or stand and give witness?

www.ingramcontent.com/pod-product-compliance
Lightning Source LLC
Chambersburg PA
CBHW051747130826
49812CB00033B/1042
* 9 7 8 9 3 7 0 9 2 1 7 3 3 *